THE CITIZEN LOBBYIST

THE CITIZEN LOBBYIST

A How-to Manual for Making
Your Voice Heard in Government

AMANDA KNIEF

Foreword by Rev. Barry W. Lynn

PITCHSTONE PUBLISING
Durham, North Carolina

Pitchstone Publishing
Durham, NC 27705
www.pitchstonepublishing.com

To contact the publisher,
please e-mail info@pitchstonepublishing.com

To contact the author,
please e-mail citizenlobbying@gmail.com

Printed in the United States of America

19 18 17 16 15 14 13   1 2 3 4 5

Library of Congress Cataloging-in-Publication Data

Knief, Amanda.
 The citizen lobbyist : a how-to manual for making your voice heard
in government / Amanda Knief ; foreword by Rev. Barry W. Lynn.
    pages cm
 Includes bibliographical references and index.
 ISBN 978-1-939578-01-3 (pbk. : alk. paper)
 1. Lobbying—United States. 2. United States—Politics and
government—2009- I. Title.
 JK1118.K55 2013
 324'.40973—dc23

                          2013004305

To Jerry Carpenter,
My eldest friend,
My Valentine's Day buddy,
I miss you every day

CONTENTS

FOREWORD

Almost everyone I know hates the decision in a Supreme Court case called *Citizens United*. It held that corporations should be treated just like people when it comes to making contributions for "independent political expenditures" to political action committees (PACs) that endorse candidates but that, at least in theory, don't coordinate their efforts with "official" campaigns. This decision has allowed a flow of vast amounts of money into campaigns from city clerk to president of the United States. In response, there have been all manner of proposals to deal with the influence of money in politics and to combat "corporate power," including amending the First Amendment to declare that corporations can be limited in giving to PACs and similar entities. The thought of all this "corporate" money unnerves many people or leads them into bouts of deep depression. You can almost hear the wailing: "We are nothing in comparison to [fill in the blank of your least favorite corporate giant]. It is unstoppable and its will shall be done in Washington no matter what we do."

The book you are about to read (maybe even take notes in the margins of) is a healthy and all-natural antidote to some of that despair. It suggests that people—real ones, not figments of the corporate imagination—can still make a difference in influencing how policies are made, whether in state legislative districts or the government located in the District of Columbia (home to senators, congresspersons, the president, and much of the federal bureaucracy).

This book is perhaps best described as a "primer" on how to influence policy—sometimes by influencing who gets elected, but more frequently, by making it clear to elected officials that you have some ideas they need to listen to. More accurately, it will guide you on how to communicate that you—and many of your closest friends, all of whom vote—have some proposals to which they should be paying due attention.

There is a dirty little secret in the world of "lobbying." It is that most people never do it. In one poll I've seen, under 20 percent of Americans have ever contacted an elected official about any topic—not the new roads in town, not the budget, not the separation of church and state, nothing. What this means is that the small percentage of people who do write a letter, dash off an e-mail, traipse to a politician's office, or pick up the phone can have a disproportionate effect on what gets done and what gets ignored. Remember, many things that "lobbyists" do are simply stopping bad, ignorant, unconstitutional, mean-spirited, or otherwise unpleasant ideas from being turned into law, regulation, or policy.

The people who do get organized in the many ways described in Amanda Knief's "how-to manual" are going to be well out in front of the curve of a politician's thinking about a topic. Yes, politicians do look at public opinion polls, but it is really easy to give a pollster your position on, say, gun control. It is a bit harder to make a well-informed case for your side of the issue and articulate it to someone else. A political figure is also likely to know that the person offering her or his opinion in a "right in the middle of dinner" telephone poll is not as likely to feel as passionately about the issue as the individual who takes the time to draft a communication with her or him or to join friends and neighbors in a direct meeting or a town hall.

I have been what is sometimes referred to as a "good guy lobbyist" for most of my life. This means I have a heartfelt reason to work in a paid position for a group that has specific goals in some arena of public affairs. (It is only people on the opposite side of the issue who consider me a "bad guy," but even they usually agree that ideological lobbyists of all stripes are at least principled.) Although it is nice for people to contribute to the social causes they care about, a yearly donation is not all that is needed for your favored position on your impassioned crusade to prevail. The employed lobbyist needs all kinds of other help, and you can deliver it. If the lobbyist is about to visit Senator Lynn (I am just making this up since I have never wanted to run for public office, and plenty of people agree with my thinking on that), it is great if the august elected official has been told by her staff that a hundred people wrote in about the topic in question in the past few days. Of course, that official probably also noticed that the local newspaper had two letters to the editor on the topic—maybe both on the side that the lobbyist is promoting. I have also often used "grasstops" people, community leaders, to bend the ear of some political person, maybe because they live in the same neighborhood or even play golf together. Coordinated "lobbying" is not always possible, of course, but it sure is nice when it is.

In the days before the Internet, I was working for the American Civil Liberties Union (ACLU). Needless to say, the very powerful Dr. James Dobson and his creation in Colorado Springs, Focus on the Family, didn't see eye-to-eye with us on much of anything (sometimes I doubted there would be agreement on the existence of the heliocentric universe). In those days, though, he had a gigantic media empire, while the ACLU was sending out "action alerts" in the mail. When Dobson wanted people to write, he told them on radio to do so, and over the next few days, bags and bags of mail would be sent to congressional offices (without even being irradiated to kill anthrax spores, something done since the 2001 anthrax letters). Believe me, it got a lot of attention.

These days, of course, the Internet has democratized things quite a bit. Every cause you care about has a Web site, sends out Facebook, Twitter, Pinterest, and Google Plus alerts, sends you e-mails to every known account, and probably produces its own radio or television programming for the Web. This makes it a great deal easier for any interested party to know what to communicate to elected officials. All this is good.

However, there is one downside to our electronic universe. Sometimes, people who care passionately about the environment search out the Facebook page of the Sierra Club, the Fund for Animals, and every other institution committing to saving the resources of the planet. They gleefully click "like" and become one of the tens of thousands of their distant "friends" who care about the same things. So far, so good, and nonprofits enjoy those "likes" too. What *The Citizen Lobbyist* does, though, is remind all of us that this kind of advocacy is only the beginning. If we want to win our case, we need to take some bigger steps to show how much we care. Joining forces on visits, with petitions, and with op-eds and letters to the editor all take us from a simple "click" to truly ground-shifting activism.

Nobody wins every battle they fight, but you are guaranteed of defeat if you assume a loss just because the other side is better funded, or is a little more tech savvy, or has fancier advertisements. When the day is done, political leaders know that every one of their constituents is a potential voter and that elections can be won or lost by a handful of votes. Treat politicians with respect, yes, but understand that they are supposed to work for their constituents (who decide on their length of employment).

—Rev. Barry W. Lynn
Executive Director, Americans United
for Separation of Church and State

PREFACE

"Being politically active does not mean yelling during campaign commercials." This is how I often start the lobbying workshops and talks I give around the country. During these events I give people from all walks of life—students, activists, senior citizens—a crash course about how to be a citizen lobbyist. I want to make it easier for people to engage their elected officials—the people we all hired by voting for them to represent us. The principle of holding our elected officials accountable to their constituents really hit home for me during my college years. I had voted in my first presidential election and began paying attention to state and local races and to issues such as college tuition, abortion rights, and LGBT rights. This was all before the events of September 11, 2001. After that tragedy, I became a true politico—watching news programs and commentary, almost obsessively—in order to understand what federal officials were doing and why. It was a confusing, scary, and exhilarating time to be paying attention to national public policy and politics.

It was also during those months and years after 9/11 that I watched federal elected officials become more isolated from the American public, and then the same distance echoed between state elected officials and their constituents. Part of the problem was simple physical access. After 9/11 and the 2001 anthrax letters that killed five people, security of government offices became much tighter. To this day, standard mail is screened so heavily and completely, there is no guaranteed date of arrival. People stayed away from their government, and elected officials did not seem to mind so much. There have been exceptions: in recent history, the 2008 presidential election of Barack Obama, and several occasions when President Obama has asked the American people to call their federal elected officials about a specific issue. In fact, in 2011, when the president told the nation to "make your voice heard" about the debt ceiling crisis, so many Americans called and e-mailed members of Congress that the Capitol's phone and Web systems crashed! The American people won the day: Congress and the president came together to agree on a (temporary) solution to the financial crisis.

However, this overwhelming interest and participation in public policy from the American public is rare. Furthermore, this was a collective response rather than an organized action around a particular outcome—it was simply aimed at getting past a stalemate in Washington, DC. A much smaller and focused lobbying effort by citizens can be effective and have measurable consequences without needing a shot of adrenaline from the president!

The basics of lobbying are to make sure your public official knows who you are, what you want, and why whatever you are seeking (action, inaction, etc.) is the best outcome. The squeaky wheel in politics gets the attention. When you are a constituent, you have the power to affect change as much as or more than any professional lobbyist, coalition, union, or industry group. This is because if you are a registered voter, you have the power to rehire—or fire—most public officials you seek action from. This guidebook is intended to help anyone who wants to have a more active role in public policy. It will teach you strategy, give you steps to take, and offer resources to help you.

You will notice that many of the examples I use in the guidebook relate to atheism and nontheistic activism. This is because most of my lobbying experience and grassroots activism have been in these areas. I have been fortunate to volunteer and collaborate with fantastic citizen and professional lobbyists all over the country, covering issues from genocide in Africa to women's reproductive rights to the environment. However, for me, providing a guidebook about being an active participant in our government is more important than getting between you and whatever issue you are passionate about. I use examples only for the purpose of illustration and not to espouse my own beliefs. Please read and use this book with this open purpose in mind.

Please let me know how this guidebook works for you—no matter your cause or interest. Whether you become a citizen lobbyist for one issue or on a regular basis, please share your stories with me. I look forward to hearing from you. E-mail me at citizenlobbying@gmail.com.

ACKNOWLEDGMENTS

I have worked hard for the career and life that I have. I believe that each person has to make her own success by making choices that facilitate opportunities. However, I would not be honest if I did not give the rather lengthy list of people that follows credit for teaching me how to find such opportunities, for inspiring confidence to take opportunities, and for supporting me in myriad ways. To those whom I have not mentioned, my apologies; you are not forgotten—I will just have to write another book!

To my publisher, Kurt Volkan, who believed in this book before I did and whose confidence in me ensured its completion.

Teachers: The future of public education is of great importance me. I think there is very little beyond the basics required to survive more than a quality education. During my matriculation there were several teachers who stood out in my memory because of the genuine interest they showed in my potential, my struggles, and my dreams. I would like to give special thanks to the following teachers: Naomi Ostby (deceased), Colleen Goodenbour (deceased), Beth McCrindle, Gene Anderson, Dr. Jane Peterson, and Barbara Mack (deceased).

Mentors: I have changed careers three times (so far) and enjoyed dabbling in various creative endeavors that have allowed me to grow and change as a person. Instrumental in encouraging me to spread my wings are those whom I call my mentors. Some are friends, some are former supervisors and coworkers—all have been selfless in offering counsel, advice, and even a gentle push to get me going. My heartfelt thanks to the following people: Kathleen Armentrout, Hector Avalos, Jennifer Bardi, Ed Buckner, Fred Edwords, Juliet Jacobs, Richard Johnson, Woody Kaplan, Lyz Liddell, Joseph McEniry, Jo Oldson, Deanna Sands, and David Silverman.

Support System: I like to think I am a self-sufficient person, but I have leaned—sometimes very heavily—on the following folks. They have borne my weight with grace and class. Thank you all for being strong when I needed strength: Cindy Banks-Radke, August Brunsman IV, R. Elisabeth Cornwell, Greta Christina, JT Eberhard, Nick Fish, David Fitzgerald, John Freutel, Dave Grzeskowiak, Jennifer Gumbel, Todd Jones,

Jenny Kalmanson, Phil Kalmanson, Teresa MacBain, Hemant Mehta, Mike Meno, Amanda Metskas, Sharon Moss, Bob Ready, Chuck Reeves, Caroline Slobodzian, and Jason Torpy.

Family: It is crucial for others to understand the importance that the support of my family has made in my life. For all that I was a "good" kid—I did not always make choices that my parents, Gene and Signe, agreed with. However, my parents never turned their backs on me and never withheld their love and pride. My siblings—Nathan, Aaron, and Amber—have sometimes looked at their big sister and said, "What are you doing?" But they, too, have always welcomed me home with open arms. Knowing that not everyone has this safe haven to turn to makes having such people in my life all the more precious to me. Thank you all for having my back.

THE CITIZEN LOBBYIST

I

WHAT IS LOBBYING?

Lobbying

Lobbying is the act of attempting to influence decisions made by officials in the government, most often elected officials and regulatory officials who are appointed to their positions.

Mayors, city council members, state legislators, U.S. senators, U.S. representatives, and the president of the United States are elected officials. However, some federal and state officials are appointed, including the heads of the departments in the executive branch, such as the secretaries of education and health and human services. Many senior officials in state executive branches—such as in the Departments of Agriculture and Labor—receive their jobs through the approval of some combination of elected officials. For example, a governor might nominate an individual to run the state Department of Revenue, but the state Senate must confirm him or her.

The appointed officials in these branches and departments are regulatory officials. However, there are also permanent employees in these branches and departments that remain in their positions no matter who is elected. Knowing who is an elected official, who is an appointed official, and who has a permanent position may affect your lobbying approach. Understanding how an official got his or her job may influence how you lobby your position on an issue. It may also provide insight about how the official will react to you or your issue when you make contact.

Advocating

Lobbying is also about advocating. This means speaking out in favor of specific public policies, issues, and even candidates for regulatory agencies and judgeships. Advocating can both be part of lobbying and be a separate activity from it. Nearly all public officials monitor their home newspaper's editorial pages as well as statewide papers. Writing a letter to the editor about an issue affecting the community or responding to someone else's letter are good ways to introduce yourself as an activist to the community and to show that your issue has a voice in the community. Writing, calling, and faxing public officials about specific issues, such as when a national organization sends out an action alert, are effective ways to team up to show the power and breadth of your issue's community. If you prefer to write your public officials, try to avoid using regular mail. Instead, send e-mail. Since the anthrax attacks, postal mail is heavily screened, which delays its delivery for unknown lengths of time. It is more efficient and reliable to send e-mail. To find local officials' contact information, try your city or county Web site. To contact state officials, try your state legislative Web site, the specific state department Web site, or the political Web site of a public official.

Another effective collaborative way to affect public policy is to attend public forums and speak when public comments are requested. At almost every level of government, there are open records and open meetings laws. These exist to keep the people's business out in the open, where the people can see what is happening, and not shut behind closed doors without witnesses and input from the public. As the Supreme Court Justice Louis Brandeis said in 1913, "Sunlight is said to be the best of disinfectants." However, if people are not paying attention, these opportunities to speak about issues ranging from zoning ordinances to birth control insurance coverage are missed. Every city, town, or borough; county or parish; and state or commonwealth will have its own set of rules and opportunities for public comment in person and in writing for laws and regulations. To find out what these are in your area, call the local office of your zoning board, city council, parish board, and state legislative office—and use their Web sites as well. The federal government also has rules that require notice of rule changes and the request for public comment. A person can go to www.regulations.gov and search for current federal rules, comments, and regulations. This is also where comments about proposed rules and regulations and changes to the same are accepted electronically. The site has a help function and will direct you to submitting comments.

Educating

Perhaps most importantly, lobbying is about educating our public officials about the multitude of issues they are going to be bombarded with. Being a public official at a federal level is a full-time job. Senators, U.S. representatives, and others have to balance the needs of the job in Washington, DC, with the needs of keeping in touch with constituents and issues in their home states and districts. Most of these elected officials have multiple offices in their home states in order to facilitate communication with local and state officials and with constituents. As elected officials, they are temporary workers who must constantly strive to keep their positions. This creates opportunities for vocal citizen lobbyists to get their attention. Contrary to public perception, the majority of public officials are not wealthy, and being an elected official alone does not make a person rich.

According to *Forbes* magazine, in 2012 the top three CEOs

earned $131.9 million, $66.65 million, and $64.40 million, respectively, for *1 year's pay*! The Speaker of the House makes about $223,500 a year. That's less than 0.18 percent of what the highest-paid CEO received in 2012. The highest-ranking member of the U.S. Senate, the Majority Leader, earns less at about $193,000. Our president earns $400,000 annually—a pittance compared to his workload and to what any major company CEO earns.

The pay doesn't get any better for a state or local elected official. The mayor of Los Angeles is the highest-paid mayor in the United States and earns only $232,000 a year. New York pays its governor the most, about $179,000. In most cities and counties around the country, being a state legislator is a part-time job or even a volunteer position. The same goes for being a mayor, city council member, school board member, or other community service position.

So how does the education aspect of lobbying come into this? It matters because a majority of our public officials spend most of their time in their official capacities as public officials in committee meetings, hearings, official functions, and legislative sessions. They rarely have time to do research—or even Google—an issue that is presented to them.

Therefore, many federal—and especially state—legislators depend heavily on lobbyists to educate them about issues: who would benefit, who would not; what are the pros and cons;

what is the background of the issue; what is happening in other states; and what is the other side's position. This system works for the most part due to trust. The lobbyists want the legislators to call them for information and to be able to give their spin; the legislators need reliable information quickly in order to make informed decisions. The lobbyists are always on the hook for providing bad information or for misleading the public official. Once burned, a lobbyist will rarely get another chance with that public official—or other public officials if word gets out that the lobbyist was unreliable or deceitful.

The reliance on lobbyists is due to the fact that few public officials have staff to do research about the many issues they will need to know about while serving. There are exceptions, but, for the most part, only large-city mayors, some state legislators (such as in Wisconsin), members of Congress, and, of course, the president and vice president have their own staff. The rest of our public officials rely on caucus staff, part-time assistance, volunteers, interns, and lobbyists.

Additionally, remember all the advocating discussed previously? According to a seminar in 2010 given by a consultant with the Congressional Progressive Caucus, about 75 percent of all U.S. congressional staff time is spent receiving, inventorying, and responding to constituent contacts. All the e-mails, phone calls, messages, and faxes are tabulated and categorized by staff so elected officials can measure how their constituents feel about every issue. This means that the research and writing about bills and issues must be fit into the remaining 25 percent of the staffs' time. It makes sense that state and local officials would track constituent contacts and feelings on issues. In fact, when I worked at the Iowa Legislature, nearly every legislator had a system for tracking constituent contacts about issues—usually by topic—and whether the constituent was pro or con.

This lack of staff power and time presents a citizen lobbyist with an opportunity to be an expert about his or her issue, that issue's community, and other tangential issues. At the local level, citizen lobbyists have the opportunity to have the most impact on public officials.

2

WHO CAN LOBBY?

Individuals

Anyone can lobby any public official in the United States. Any citizen or permanent resident has the right to lobby his or her elected officials about issues of concern on their own behalf. If a person is lobbying on behalf of a third party and is being paid to do so, he or she will likely have to register with the state or federal government (for guidelines, see the section "Professional Lobbyists and Lobbying Organizations").

There are no limits on how many letters (or e-mails) can be written, phone calls can be placed, or visits can be made by an individual. (However, do be aware of stalking and harassment laws in your state—no one wants a second shadow!) Individuals may lobby alone or with others. Be aware that if your group is large enough, you may be classified as a protest and may need a permit. It is always a good idea to check the Web site of the place (e.g., statehouse, U.S. Capitol) you will be visiting for any instructions or to call ahead to let them know you are coming.

Groups

Groups of unaffiliated people (friends, family, survivors of cancer, bicycle safety advocates, etc.) may work together to lobby. However, any group that is registered as a 501(c)(3) nonprofit organization is limited in the amount of lobbying it can do as an official organization. The Internal Revenue Service (IRS) states that no such organization may qualify for nonprofit status if a substantial part of its activities are "attempting to influence legislation."

The IRS defines "legislation" as

> action by Congress, any state legislature, any local council, or similar governing body, with respect to acts, bills, resolutions, or similar item (such as legislative confirmation of appointive office), or by the public in referendum, ballot initiative, constitutional amendment, or similar procedure. It does not include actions by executive, judicial, or administrative bodies.

This means that a nonprofit organization will be considered to have violated its nonprofit status if a substantial part of its members' activities on behalf of the organization can be regarded as trying to influence legislation or urging citizens to contact public officials for the purpose of influencing legislation—or if the organization advocates a position on specific legislation.

This doesn't mean that nonprofit organizations can't be part of the public policy conversation. The IRS clearly states on its Web site that "organizations may conduct educational meetings, prepare and distribute educational materials, or otherwise consider public policy issues in an educational manner without jeopardizing their tax-exempt status."

The educational aspect can be widely interpreted. For example, the Kansas City Atheist Coalition hosted a public debate about same-sex marriage in September 2012. Iowa Atheists and Freethinkers hosted a lunchtime educational program at the Iowa Statehouse about the fallacies of intelligent design in 2010. American Atheists was welcomed to the city of Des Moines by Mayor Frank Cownie at the beginning of its national convention in 2011. The Triangle Freethought Society hosted a breakfast social for local public officials during its 2012 National Day of Reason celebration. Dozens of such groups have found myriad ways to bring social issues and public officials together without endorsing political candidates or particular issues, yet still raise consciousness between government and the nontheistic movement.

However, lobbying to some degree is allowed even for

501(c)(3) nonprofit organizations. The IRS measures the amount of lobbying and how much is OK with two tests. The first is known as the "substantial part test." Under this test, a 501(c)(3) nonprofit organization's attempts to influence legislation should not constitute a "substantial part of its overall activities." This is the trickier test of the two because there is no way to quantify what level of lobbying is permissible. Rather, the IRS states that it "considers a variety of factors, including the time devoted (by both compensated and volunteer workers) and the expenditures devoted by the organization to the activity, when determining whether the lobbying activity is substantial."

This test allows large national organizations to employ a lobbyist as part of their overall operations. This allowance also allows smaller local groups to engage in smaller targeted lobbying efforts. For example, Iowa Atheists and Freethinkers for several years sent letters to every member of the Iowa Legislature to protest the prayers said at the beginning of each session day and the stipend and mileage allowance given to the clergy who perform the prayers.

The second test, the "expenditure test," is more definitive and is a better option for groups whose members know that they will be doing lobbying on a regular basis and want both the group and the IRS to be able to measure the lobbying so both parties know what the limit is. In order to qualify, a group must elect for the expenditure test under 501(h). This test allows a group to spend a specified amount of its income on lobbying based on its total expenditures. For example, if a group has $500,000 or less in expenditures for a given tax year, as of 2012, the maximum amount of lobbying expenditure allowed would be $100,000, or 20 percent of total expenditures.

Professional Lobbyists and Lobbying Organizations

The federal government and each state has its own regulations for paid lobbyists—or for those who are acting on behalf of a third party. At the federal level there are two kinds of regulations: for domestic lobbyists and for foreign lobbyists. Foreign entities seeking to "influence U.S. public opinion, policy, and laws" must register under the Foreign Agents Registration Act (FARA) of 1938. FARA covers foreign political parties, any person or organization from outside the United States (except U.S. citizens), and any entity created under the laws of a foreign country or having its principle business in a foreign country. Trying to affect policy in the United States is quite popular. According to the December 2011 FARA report by the Attorney General to Congress, more than 138 countries had registered foreign agents in the United States.

Domestic lobbyists are also regulated by the federal government. While the tax code restricts the lobbying activities of 501(c)(3) nonprofit organizations, the Lobbying Disclosure

Act (LDA), 2 U.S.C. § 1605 regulates who is a lobbyist, what is a lobbying activity, and what must be reported to the government. Below are a few highlights of the distinctions between professional lobbying and lobbying by private citizens (please note that this is not a comprehensive list):

- According to the LDA, the president, the vice president, and any elected member of Congress are "covered officials."
- The LDA covers any oral or written communication to any covered official made on behalf of a *client*.
- The LDA covers those communications that meet bullet 1 and bullet 2, *and* are related to the formulation, modification, or adoption of federal legislation, federal rules, executive orders, or administration of a federal program or policy.
- The LDA states that the request for a meeting with a covered official is NOT a lobbying contact.
- The LDA states that submitting comments about policy after the government solicits public input is NOT a lobbying contact.

State Lobbying Registrations

Every state and the District of Columbia has some kind of official registration for lobbyists. The registration requirements vary from simply requiring the lobbyist's name and professional information (about ten states) to requiring a recent photo (in as many as nine states) to requiring fees (in more than thirty states and starting as high as $750 in Texas). Some states don't require that a lobbyist receive compensation (such as payment) in order to qualify as a lobbyist. However, these states all seem to have exemptions for those who lobby and receive only reimbursement of expenses (such as in Virginia). It is important that anyone who is seeking to become an activist read the relevant state statutes to be sure he or she is following state law. You will be able to find this information on the relevant state Web page—usually run by the secretary of state or the state board of elections. I have included a Resource Guide at the end of this guidebook that includes the Web sites for the relevant authorities who regulate lobbyists and elections in each state.

Why You Are Not a Professional Lobbyist

Inevitably questions arise from activists who lobby as volunteers for organizations and on behalf of issues they care about on a regular basis about whether they have accidentally become professional lobbyists. In almost every case, the answer is no.

In order to be a professional lobbyist and be required to register with the federal government and most state governments as such, you must be lobbying for compensation on behalf of a client. Volunteers do not qualify no matter how many trips they make to a legislator or to Washington, DC. Even interns for college or graduate school whose responsibilities may include public policy work and lobbying will likely be exempt from lobbying registration because of the lack of compensation or the exemptions most states provide. It is wise to check the appropriate state statute because every situation is different. However, if you are a private citizen seeking to talk to your public official about an issue or public policy of concern to you, you have nothing to worry about.

3

FOCUSING ON AND IDENTIFYING ISSUES FOR LOBBYING

There is no shortage of issues that a citizen lobbyist may want to become involved in, whether related to gun control (or preventing gun laws), the environment, disappearing bees, the separation of church and state, public education reform, LGBT rights, vaccine awareness, health care law, women's issues, defense spending, farm subsidies, closing Guantanamo Bay, voting reform, legalizing marijuana, repealing the death penalty, animal rights, juvenile justice reform, international rights issues—and the list goes on. There are countless issues at the international, national, state, and local levels that you may want to bring to the attention of your public officials.

But with so many issues swirling around to care about, you may feel like you are shouting into the wind. Part of being an effective citizen lobbyist is identifying the best way to approach a public official about your issue. Sometimes the head-on approach won't work because there isn't enough public interest or the issue is too controversial. But there are some ways to get your issue the attention you believe it deserves.

For federal, national, and international issues, watch the legislation that is introduced in the House and Senate. Less than 5 percent of all the bills introduced in the House and Senate in 2012 actually made it to the president for signing (or veto), but that didn't stop the members of Congress from filing bills on topics ranging from homeless children to a coin commemorating Ronald Reagan. These bills can be monitored for free on the Library of Congress's Web site, THOMAS, which tracks federal legislation and action. Knowing what topics are important enough for a member of Congress to sponsor a bill will help you learn who will be interested in your issue. THOMAS will also provide information about who cosponsored bills and what amendments every member of Congress offered. Monitoring your members of Congress's legislative action is vital to any activist's plan to push an issue forward.

News sites such as *Politico* and *Mother Jones* also closely follow and report on federal political news. Of course MSNBC, CNN, and Fox News can be relied on to have loud headlines and breaking political news. But news shows are usually covering up-to-the-minute news, which does not always work well with planning for lobbying.

For state legislators, monitor your state's legislative Web site. Every state has a site that gives information about the current legislative session, the bills being considered, and other information about committee hearings and votes. Bringing your issue up to a public official out of the blue will rarely get it the kind of attention and action you want it to receive. Learning how the legislature works and who would handle your issue are critical steps in preparing to lobby.

Local issues can be targeted through local news sources, especially newspapers and their Web sites. The letters-to-the-editor section and op-ed pages are great places to find out what the community in general is thinking and talking about. Responding to a particular letter to the editor or op-ed is a great way to get your point-of-view published. Just be sure to check the guidelines that the newspapers may have concerning length, style, or your contact information. If a newspaper is going to publish your letter, someone from the editorial board is going to contact you to confirm you sent in the letter.

Of course today there is the advantage of social media. Many public officials as well as government offices have Facebook pages, e-newsletters, Web sites, and Twitter accounts. Monitoring any or all of these may allow you to find out about policy decisions, new issues, or controversies before the general public—or to pick up on an issue that the news media may miss or not pay attention to.

Finally, don't discount your own experiences and those of your friends and family in your citizen lobbying efforts. While it would not be wise to pontificate in a lobbying meeting about your personal ideas or to write a manifesto to be sent to a public official about how to approach fixing a particular problem, anecdotal evidence can be powerful, especially when it comes firsthand. Sharing experiences of discrimination, miseducation, abuse, successes, and good outcomes and information about the issue community in general can help a public official empathize with you and understand your point of view.

4

WHO IS THE RIGHT PUBLIC OFFICIAL FOR THE ISSUE?

Who you lobby is just as important as the issue you are lobbying about. The first thing to be sure of is that you are a constituent of whomever you want to meet with. This of course does not apply to regulatory officials, but it does to anyone who is elected to office. Most elected officials or their staff members will ask for your name and address prior to a meeting in order to verify you are a constituent. If you are organizing a lobby day and have several persons from different areas who want or need to lobby together, that is perfectly fine. Just be sure that in every meeting there is at least one legitimate constituent for each public official. These officials or their staffs are giving you time out of their schedules, so don't lie or mislead them about who is coming to the meeting.

If the only constituent in a group cancels, be ready to call the elected official's office to cancel the meeting.

How do you decide whom to talk to: the governor, a state legislator, mayor, a zoning board member, or a U.S. senator? The decision depends on who will be affected most by the issue you choose and where the issue affects people. If the issue is local, talk to local officials; if it is national, talk to federal officials. The key is to be able to tell any elected officials you talk to how embracing your issue or your side of an issue will affect their constituents or how it will affect the area represented by the public officials.

If you are targeting regulatory officials, such as the head of the U.S. Health and Human Services Department, about a policy that is open for public comment, be sure to state why you personally are writing and want the policy to go your way. If you can provide facts to back your position or other evidence that supports why your position would also be best for others, be sure to include that as well. If you have a meeting with a regulatory official, you should be ready to discuss your reasons and have them ready to present.

Here is a list of just some of the public officials you can lobby:

- President of the United States

- Vice President of the United States

- Secretaries of all Cabinet positions—Labor, Education,

Health and Human Services, Veterans Affairs, State, etc.—
and all of the lower-level officials in their departments

- U.S. senators (two per state)
- U.S. representatives; delegates from the District of Columbia, American Samoa, Guam, the U.S. Virgin Islands, and the Northern Mariana Islands; and the Resident Commissioner from Puerto Rico
- State governors
- Mayors
- State legislators
- Heads of all the state departments and the lower-ranking officials
- City councils, planning boards, alderman, etc.
- Zoning boards
- School boards
- Elected judges
- Elected law enforcement, such as sheriffs

As of January 2011, 38 percent of the members of Congress claimed in their official biographies to have held at least one public office at the state or local level before being elected to federal office. With so many members of the federal legislature having served at the state and local levels, it is ideal for a citizen lobbyist to get to know his or her local and state public officials—and for them to get to know you. It is much easier to lobby and educate officials in your own backyard than to have to trek to Washington, DC, to do it.

Do not limit who you lobby by party, gender, or voting record. While such categorization is helpful in identifying potential allies for specific issues, don't rule out public officials who on paper wouldn't appear receptive to your issue. To do so would mean automatically giving up on almost half of our public officials at almost any level of government on almost any given issue. No activist or issue community can afford to write off or ignore half of the political community if they want to gain true political and social progress for their issue.

If there is a public official who is not on your side on your issue or if your particular representative does not seem to be representing you, find an issue or idea that you do have in common—and start lobbying with that (even if it is not your true lobbying goal). For example, if my goal is to stop religious prayers during city council meetings, but my city council representative supports prayers during council meetings, as a citizen lobbyist I may not want to start lobbying him or her on that issue. Instead, it would be better to find an issue that we have in common. I would then research and make an appointment with the councilperson about that issue. In this example, let's say that the common issue is that we both support community development and that there is a vote for new bike trails coming before the council. I, as a citizen lobbyist, might schedule a meeting with my council representative about the vote on the bike trails, thank the councilperson for his or her efforts, and ask what can be done to improve cyclists' safety or for more trails, or something related to the topic. At the end of the meeting, I would thank the councilperson or staffer again, and say, "I really appreciate you meeting with me. I look forward to sharing this discussion with my friends at my [Local Atheists & Freethinkers Group]—many of them ride with me on the weekends and we will all be at the council meeting for the vote."

It is likely that the councilperson or the staffer will be surprised to hear the citizen lobbyist is a member of a group with interests counter to the official's. It may stun him or her that a pleasant meeting took place and the subject of religion never came up. It is an innocuous way to introduce the idea that nonreligious folks are also represented by this councilperson. It is unlikely it will have an immediate impact, but it allows for, in this case, two persons with opposing views to meet on a common issue. It is a first step to introducing the issue that is the final goal of the citizen lobbyist. Building relationships takes time, and this is a good way to start to do this. Perhaps the next meeting the citizen lobbyist would make with this councilperson would be about offering a nonreligious message instead of a prayer at a council meeting.

No matter who you lobby or what issue you lobby, the most valuable element of citizen lobbying is making the connection with your public official. Putting a face to your issue for that official or staffer is a big step in humanizing your issue, making it more personal for him or her, and making you part of the public policy discussion.

5

WHO, IF ANYONE,
DO YOU LOBBY WITH?

―――――――

You can always lobby by yourself with public officials. One-on-one lobbying is effective and always allows you to communicate your story directly with your chosen public official. This means you can choose the method, the time, the place—you have complete control over your lobbying contact and message. However, this also means you also bear the entire burden—setting up the meeting, deciding on your message. Doing it all may be overwhelming, especially the first few times you do it.

Lobbying as part of a small group is also an effective method for communicating with your chosen public official and allows you to distribute the responsibilities among the group. When several people lobby together, they can be from different districts or states so that they may visit multiple representatives in a short time. Just be sure that there's at least one constituent in your group for every elected official you meet with.

A third option is to collaborate with other groups who have a similar interest in the issue you seek to lobby about. For example, if you were going to lobby about women's right to contraceptives, you might contact the local Planned Parenthood, the local American Civil Liberties Union, a local chapter of Americans United for Separation of Church and State, a chapter of the Secular Coalition for America, and/ or a local chapter of the National Organization for Women to ask if their members would be interested in organizing a larger lobbying effort. The benefits of this are many. First, your group will be able to network with new people who may not have known your group existed. Second, your lobbying efforts may be increased with an influx of new energy, new people, and more experience. Third, your group gains credibility just by being associated with more established groups who are known for lobbying and grassroots efforts. The potential for collaboration and knowledge sharing is limitless.

6

FIRST CONTACT: SETTING UP A MEETING

Citizen lobbying is all about the face-to-face meeting with your public official. The meeting provides you, the citizen lobbyist, with the opportunity to connect with his or her public official—and the public official gets the opportunity (or is forced) to listen to what his or her constituent wants. The whole process starts with the citizen lobbyist making first contact by phone or e-mail. Depending upon which public official you are trying to reach, one method or the other may be more optimal. For example, trying to call any Iowa legislator at the Statehouse through the official switchboard is almost impossible. The legislators' individual phones are in the Senate and House chambers, so they don't ring—rather, a small light flashes when someone calls. No one answers the phones and it may be days before anyone gets your voice message. However, the Iowa legislators do pay close attention to their e-mail—as do their part-time clerks. This makes e-mail the optimal way to ask for an appointment during the legislative session with a legislator in Iowa. Doing a little research about the communication methods of your public official can mean the difference between getting a meeting and never hearing a word back.

Keep timing in mind as well. The U.S. Congress is constantly in-session, but it takes frequent breaks. In fact, during the 112th Congress (2011–2012), the U.S. House took every fourth week off as a "constituent week" so representatives could go back home and connect with people in their districts. State legislatures (also known as general assemblies and general courts) operate differently. Some meet once every two years to vote on legislation, some meet year-round in block sessions, some meet for a set number of days each year, and so on. It is important that you know how your state legislature operates if you are going to lobby someone who is elected to it.

The Resource Guide at the end of this guidebook includes the Web site information for all fifty state legislatures and the council for the District of Columbia. Use the sites to learn the schedule of your legislature—and decide whether it is better to approach your public official when the legislature is in-session, in recess, or off-session.

Once you decide whether to call or e-mail, keep a record—especially if you are contacting more than one public official—so you don't forget who you contacted (the official, the scheduler, the assistant, etc.), when you called or sent the message, and, if you called, whether you left a message. If you don't receive a response after 2–3 business days, call or e-mail again and gently state this is your second attempt to schedule a meeting—writing or reciting back the details about the first attempt. As you follow-up, be persistent but not annoying. Remember, public officials and their staffs get sick, go on vacation, take maternity and paternity leave, quit, and get fired. There may be good reasons why someone doesn't get back to you immediately. If you get demanding and rude, whoever does finally get your message(s) will be much less likely to help you.

7

WHAT?! I DON'T GET TO MEET THE BIG KAHUNA?

———————

Despite the frequent references in this guide to "meeting with your public official," chances are you will be meeting with a staff member or "staffer." This is true at all levels of government, from local to federal. Most public officials just don't have time to meet with constituents (at least not outside fundraisers and other expensive events). However, you might be surprised which public officials you will get a direct appointment to see.

- The mayors of small- and medium-size towns will likely meet with you themselves, as will members of city councils in those size towns. They won't have the staff to meet with you, and they want active constituents to feel that they are getting personal attention.

- State legislators often meet directly with the constituents, especially in those states such as Iowa that do not provide their legislators with personal staff.

- Elected sheriffs—just like elected mayors—want their constituents to feel their concerns are being personally addressed, and thus they want to meet with their active constituents. It's also difficult to delegate this kind of responsibility onto the deputies who usually stay in their positions no matter who the sheriff is.

- Mid- to upper-level officials at regulatory agencies, state and federal, will meet with you. You aren't likely to get a meeting with the U.S. secretary of state— but an undersecretary is possible. This is because constituents, especially active ones, usually vote, and regulatory officials' jobs are dependent on whoever is president or governor staying in office. Complaints, controversies, and constituent unrest are all bad for the incumbent—and excellent ways to maneuver a meeting.

However, meeting with a staffer is not something to despair over. It can be to your advantage. As discussed earlier, 75 percent of all staffer time at the federal level is spent on sorting and responding to constituent contacts. This leaves 25 percent of staffer time for researching and writing about actual issues and legislation. It leaves little time for any of them to be experts about the issue you are lobbying about. The same will be true for your public official; it is more likely you will know more about the issue than the public official you meet with. You will be the expert and in a great position to influence the staffer or public official about the issue. However, do so with caution. Your value and influence go only as far as you are trusted. So providing accurate and unbiased information is important to being a quality citizen lobbyist.

You will not likely be the expert when meeting with officials from regulatory agencies, which have a much narrower focus and whose employees have a similar focus. However, you will have the advantage of being the expert on your perspective. Again, be accurate and don't misrepresent yourself or the other side's arguments. Being well-received is all about credibility.

No matter who you meet with, it is important to have your facts straight, to know the other side's arguments, and to be able to articulate why your position is the better one—and especially how it benefits the constituents of the public official (or administration) you are meeting with.

8

TRUST AND RELIABILITY DETERMINE ISSUE SUCCESS

From understanding the issue to knowing the background of the public official you are meeting with, preparation is the most important part of the lobbying visit. Going to a meeting ill-prepared is worse than not lobbying at all. You will have wasted the public official's time, come across as unprofessional, and left a negative impression not only in relation to the issue but also of the issue community.

Research the Issue

Each person who plans to attend a lobbying meeting should do his or her own research. Take time to do an Internet search about the issue, read Web news, find a Wikipedia article. Next, be sure you know something about each public official you will be meeting with—even if your meeting is with a staffer. For a federal legislator, the Library of Congress maintains a record of all congressional votes, introduced bills, and other legislative action on its Web site THOMAS. Almost every elected official—federal, state, and local—has his or her own official Web site, which will contain information about issue positions and votes. Each state has a legislative Web site that tracks all the bills considered by the legislators—including who sponsored which bills and the votes. Don't forget to look at social media either, such as Facebook pages, Twitter, and e-newsletters.

Lobbying Papers

You or someone in your group should prepare a "leave-behind" for each lobbying meeting you will attend: one leave-behind per meeting. A leave-behind is a single sheet of paper or a folder with information about the issue you are lobbying about and the basics about the group you are representing, as applicable.

If you are solo lobbying, you might attach a business card with your name and contact information. If you are lobbying as part of an organized lobbying day with a lobbying organization, you will likely be provided information about that group and the issue(s) you will be presenting, so you will not have to prepare anything yourself. If you are part of a nonprofit organization whose primary purpose is not lobbying (this includes all 501(c)(3) organizations), your group will need to decide if the lobbying visit is an official function of the organization before passing out information about the group during the lobbying meeting.

The information about the issue that you provide the public official is known as a lobbying paper. It should be basic, simply including a few facts that summarize the issue, a statement that gives your point of view, and a declarative statement that includes "the ask"—what it is that you want from the public official. The lobbying paper should not be more than a page (maybe a page and a half—using the front and back). You want the public official to have something educational and tangible to take away from the meeting, but remember, no one has time to read a dissertation. Forcing yourself to keep the lobbying paper short will also help you formulate your talking points for the meeting.

An example of a one-page lobbying paper is provided in Appendix I. Personal or group information can be added to the beginning or the end. If there are additional materials that are relevant to the issue or the group, such as a brochure, using a folder to house the materials is appropriate. Be sure to use a bold and clear label on the folder so it is easy for the public official to identify.

Have a Dress Rehearsal

Whether you are going alone or with a group, practice what you will say and how you will say it before you go. Have someone pretend to be the public official or staffer so you have the opportunity to anticipate a real conversation. Be sure to practice a meeting with a friendly public official or staffer and a meeting with someone who is skeptical or even slightly hostile. Both are possible, even likely, to occur.

If there will be two or more people lobbying, practice who will take what parts of the discussion. Not everyone has to have a speaking role, but anyone who wants to speak should be given the opportunity. If meeting with a public official or staffer, at least one constituent needs to be actively involved in the conversation, though others in the group not represented may also take active roles. A sample lobbying visit conversation is provided in Appendix II. Feel free to use it as a guide, but your lobbying issue will dictate changes in the conversation. It should not be used as a script.

Human Nature

What you don't say in a lobby meeting can be as important or more important as the discussion itself—and how you convey your message is even more important than the words. According to Alton Barbour and Mele Koneya, authors of *Louder than Words: Nonverbal Communication*, the words that you use will account for only 7 percent of your message's total impact. The tone, volume, and pitch of your voice will account for 38 percent of your message's total impact. Finally, your body movements and facial expressions will account for the remaining 55 percent of your message's total impact.

Therefore, no matter what you or those with you say during the lobby meeting, be attentive during the conversation, avoid negative facial expressions, and do not gaze around the room when someone in your group or the staffer or public official is speaking. Posture is key to conveying confidence in your message—sitting up straight and facing the staffer or public official is vital. Slumping or laying your head on your hand indicates defeat—not the message you want to convey in a lobby meeting!

Equally important, make direct eye contact. It's essential for making a good impression. If you are uncomfortable looking directly into someone's eyes when engaged in conversation, the solution is to focus your eyes somewhere else on the person's face. For example, train your eyes on the person's nose or mouth. As long as your focus is somewhere on the face, the person with whom you are speaking will perceive that you are looking in his or her eyes.

Bowties Are Cool

Whether you are meeting with the mayor of a town with thirty-two residents or a U.S. senator, be sure to dress appropriately. This does not mean you must wear a business suit. This is true for women and men. It does mean nice pants or slacks, skirt, or dress; a button-down shirt or blouse; and closed-toe shoes. You should be comfortable, but you also want to show you take the meeting, the lobbying issue, and yourself seriously. So don't wear jeans, shorts, T-shirts, flip-flops, or hats, and don't let your bra straps show. If it sounds a bit strict and conservative, it is. Notice I did not say anything about tattoos, hair color, piercings, jewelry, or lapel pins or buttons. You should be free to express yourself and be who you are, but give yourself the best opportunity by dressing in a way that says, "This issue is important to me."

9

THE VISIT:
10 THINGS TO REMEMBER

───────────

You're finally headed to the lobbying meeting you have been preparing for. Be sure to follow these ten important tips.

1. Be nice to the gatekeeper.

This is true for whoever greets you at a public official's office. Whether you are greeted by a secretary, office manager, doorkeeper, receptionist, or security officer, be friendly and courteous. Not only is it the polite thing to do, but doing so makes a good first impression. Don't assume that whoever is first to greet you is less important than the public official or staffer you are going to meet. I have seen elected officials handle the front office when office personnel were not available, been greeted by a senator's chief of staff covering the phones over lunch, and met a mayor's spouse when I stopped by at the end of the day for an appointment.

2. Introduce yourself and allow others in the group to do the same.

One of purposes of the meeting is to allow constituents to interact with the public official or staffer. Even if not everyone in the group wants to have an active role in the conversation about the issue you are visiting about, it is important that each person have the opportunity to introduce themselves and shake the hand of whoever you are meeting. Personal contact cements conversations and increases the impact of your visit. Simply introducing everyone yourself does not have the same impact and gives the impression that the others in the group are less important.

3. Thank the public official, staffer, or regulatory official for something the public official or regulatory agency has done, even if not related to the issue you are lobbying about.

This is a good idea especially when the public official (or staffer) with whom you are meeting is not on your side of the issue you are visiting about. It is a shortcut to establishing common ground and requires that you do some research ahead of time. For example, if you are visiting a state legislator who is less likely to be on your side about the issue of minimum wage increases, but voted in the past on the issue of education in a way that supports your views, bring up the education vote and thank the legislator for his or her vote and support on that issue. Successful citizen lobbying is predicated on trust and activism; the more you can show you know public policy and that you are paying attention, the more importance your opinion on your issue will carry over time.

4. Make friends with the public official, regulatory official, or staffer.

Small talk is an art and one that not many people are naturally gifted with; most of us have to learn it. This step can come before step 3 if it seems natural in the conversation. Again, this is another shortcut to creating common ground with the public official (or staffer) with whom you are meeting. As a lobbyist, I always followed the major national sports— not because I am a huge fan, but because for most men in politics sports are a common language. Being able to speak intelligently about a sport—and knowing how an elected official's home professional or collegiate team is doing—can be a great conversation starter. It also is good to know something about the home district or state of any federal elected official you are going to speak to.

There are only a handful of states I have not visited, so I always have a story about visiting a state ready when I meet a senator. For the few states I have not visited, I have researched notable places I would like to visit that are true to me. I don't ever lie when I am making small talk—it is all part of building relationships. So if you are not a skier, don't talk about skiing with an elected official from Colorado—choose something else from the state that interests you. Often when I share this particular step, I get the questions, "Why do this?" and "Why waste the time getting to know a staffer?"

Each question has its own answer. First, I do this because I want the public official (or staffer) to see me as a person, not just another lobbyist. I want them to know I cared enough about the meeting to really pay attention to where the elected official was coming from. I want to try to start building that relationship—and that is the answer to why it is not a waste of time.

Unless you are a one-time citizen lobbyist, you will likely be back to your elected official's office again about the same issue—or even about another one. Treating the person you are meeting as a fellow human being and not just as an obstacle to get through is good public relations. Thinking longer term, you don't know where this person will end up—if a staffer, maybe he or she will run for office someday; if a state legislator, maybe he or she will run for U.S. Congress. A little effort to forge a relationship now could have a big payoff later.

5.   Ask for the public official's position on the issue or the regulatory agency's timing for an issue.

Whether you are meeting with the elected official or the staffer, ask for the elected official's position on your issue. You likely won't get an answer from a staffer, who will say something about not speaking for the official. If you are meeting with the elected official, try to get them on the record—always. If you are meeting with a regulatory official about a policy issue, ask for the timing of a decision on the issue. Try to get a deadline. You probably won't, but pushing is OK. Just push politely.

6.   Make an action request.

Even if it is in your lobbying paper, you still need to bring up your "ask" in the meeting. This way you have the opportunity to see how the public official or staffer reacts, and he or she will have the opportunity to follow up with questions to be sure he or she understands what you are requesting. Don't expect an answer one way or the other—most likely the public official or staffer will take it under consideration, or the staffer will take it to the official for his or her consideration.

7.   Maintain composure.

It is hard to mess up being a citizen lobbyist. I always tell my audiences the two ways to know that you blew it are if you have been pepper sprayed or are being led away in handcuffs.

Otherwise, you probably did great. However, that's not to say it will be easy to handle yourself with dignity and speak respectfully to every public official with whom you meet. You need to be the better person though. You have more to lose than the public official or staffer.

At a 2012 national lobbying event in Washington, DC, my friend JT Eberhard took the plunge and lobbied for an afternoon. JT is one of the most honest and forthright people I have ever met. He tweeted after lobbying that he would never do it again because he was afraid he would end up biting through his tongue. JT's lobbying meetings were less cordial than what most people experience, but he showed extreme grace by holding back his personal feelings and allowing the lobbying process to continue for the entire group.

8.   Collect business cards.

Whether you are meeting with a local, state, or federal public official—or his or her staffer—each will have business cards. Collect them like lottery tickets. It can be difficult to find direct contact information for staffer and public officials, so if it is offered or you can ask for it in person—get it. You can also bring your own cards to a meeting. Creating a card for your forays as a citizen lobbyist is perfectly appropriate. Be sure to only put information on the card that you want to be made public. Also, don't put the name of your employer or the name of an organization to which you belong on it without proper permission. Adding an employer or organization to a card could imply you are lobbying on behalf of your employer or the organization.

9. No kibitzing until you leave the building.

Kibitzing means to chat or talk informally—or to gossip. If you are in a group, don't talk about how good or bad the meeting was while you are still in the building—continue to act professionally. If you are alone, likewise, don't whip out your phone to call someone to dish about the meeting while still in government offices or hallways. Wait until you are out of the building and can't be overheard by others inside. You never know who could overhear that you just met with the mayor about issue X or with Representative Smith about issue Z. Most meetings with private citizens and lobbyists are known only to the public official's office staff.

10. Follow-up with a thank-you e-mail.

Be sure to send a thank-you e-mail to each person you met with about your issue within twenty-four hours of the meeting. For all the reasons covered previously, regular mail is not the best choice for communication with public officials. The timing is important because if you wait too long, the public official or staffer will have forgotten the meeting you are referring to. The e-mail is a good reminder for him or her to do his or her own follow-up on your issue.

10

ELECTIONS

Voting

If you are interested in being a citizen lobbyist the first and most important step to take is to vote—in every election. A representative democracy is dependent upon its citizens using their power at the ballot to effect change at the most basic level—and at every level of government. This is a power that too many people dismiss as ineffectual, diluted by too many people, unimportant due to the electoral college (in presidential elections), or just uninteresting.

I won't go into the pluses and minuses of the Electoral College; others have taken on this subject in-depth. There are also plenty of experts to discuss why one person, one vote, and universal suffrage are still battles we are fighting today in the United States. However, voting is an invaluable resource for a citizen lobbyist because it requires you to learn about the school board, the zoning commission, the city council, the mayoral candidates, and so on. Paying attention to elections means you are paying attention to campaigns and what potential elected officials are offering as your hired representative in government. It is much harder to go back and try to find that information after the fact than it is to find it as it is happening. Local news stations, newspapers, and online sources will not cover local and state campaigns in the same detail national campaigns are covered. Additionally, few local and state candidates have the resources to get their messages out the way national candidates do.

If you are going to be a citizen lobbyist, one of the best things you can have in your lobbying arsenal is a regular voting record that can be verified by anyone who bothers to look for it. Most states allow a person's voter registration information, including name, address, and phone number, to be public information. Also, your party affiliation (or lack thereof) and voting history may also be accessible—for free or for a small fee. In Florida, for example, as of January 2013, for $5 the state will mail anyone who requests it a disk with voter registration information. In Iowa, the law allows the state to sell voter registration information. This information is controlled individually by the states, usually by the secretary of state or another state-level official, but some states use a state election board to regulate elections and voting procedures and information. However, in every state your vote itself is private—no one will know who you did or didn't vote for. But whether you voted or not can be accessible. So when you become a citizen lobbyist and you start making noise about wanting your elected official to work on your issue, it is helpful to have credibility as an established voter should someone go looking—and that means in every election, not just in the "big" national elections.

Campaigns: Participating

Many people who have never participated in any kind of political campaign think participating is less to be excited about than scheduling a root canal. For those who have volunteered or worked for a campaign, the experience is often quite different. It is energizing to be around people who are excited about issues, public policy, and—of course—a candidate. Being a part of a campaign means being on the front lines of learning voter turnout strategies, collaboration techniques, and cooperation skills. It means the fun and craziness of interacting with the public—and having "war" stories to share with others years later. It is an experience that provides new perspective to politics. For a citizen lobbyist, there are two specific reasons and ways to get involved in political campaigns and, depending on your goals, one or the other will be more helpful to you and your issue.

If you are lobbying for an issue that is relatively unknown or the candidates for the office(s) in the current election have not gone on the record about, it is often a good strategy to try to get these candidates to answer a question about your issue. You can go about this indirectly through a questionnaire that you send to the candidates. Many state and national organizations have done this and continue to send such surveys to candidates to get an overall picture of the candidates' views on particular issues. However, there is no guarantee the candidates will answer the particular question or even return your survey.

Candidates for every office usually host some kind of public forum where the public is allowed to ask questions. These can be chats at a local restaurant or formal question-and-answer sessions. Be prepared with several questions about your issue and don't be afraid to be the first person to ask a question. You don't know how long the candidate will take questions or when something might happen to end the session. If you can, take a friend to record you asking the question and the candidate's answer. You can do it yourself, but engaging the candidate and paying attention to the answer should be your focus.

If you can get video, that is best because it will show the whole scene. No matter how the candidate answers—good, bad, ugly—you will have a record and can use it to gain attention to your issue. This has worked numerous times for groups and persons advocating issues that might not otherwise have gotten attention.

For example, I attended a presidential town hall meeting at the University of Maryland in July 2011 when I worked for the Secular Coalition for America. The topic was a new jobs initiative that President Obama was going to introduce. I came prepared with a tangential question. The president called on me first during the question and answer portion, and I asked him to explain how, after he had promised during his 2008 presidential campaign to end religious discrimination in hiring practices by faith-based groups that received government funds and in an economy where the average person was struggling to find a job based on skills, he could justify allowing a woman to be refused a job because of her religious beliefs or lack thereof. President Obama—a former constitutional law professor and one of the best public speakers we have ever had in office— then fumbled for more than three minutes to answer. I didn't have to record the exchange—it was broadcast live on C-SPAN and the Internet.

The question and answer with the president was the first time anyone had been able to get President Obama to publicly discuss faith-based discrimination policies since he had been elected president. The question had the added effect of leading the mainstream media to bring up the issue—from the

Huffington Post to CNN—and of course see it widely covered by the nontheistic and religious news and blog sources.

YouTube and other video-sharing sites are great tools for spreading the words of political candidates after you get them to talk about your issue. As discussed earlier, many national and federal public officials begin their careers in local and state offices. Reaching these officials when a citizen lobbyist has easier access and when these officials are less likely to consider the future consequences of being honest about how they feel about your issue are fantastic reasons to get local and state public officials on the record about your issue as soon as you can.

Of course, sometimes there is no question about where a candidate or incumbent sits on an issue. If one candidate would clearly be better in an elected office than one or more other candidates, then it is a great option for a citizen lobbyist to actually volunteer or work for a campaign. There are a dozen ways to assist in a campaign—and each campaign will have different needs. For a citizen lobbyist, keep the following goals in mind. First, you want people in the campaign to know why you are volunteering for the campaign—that you believe this candidate will be good for your issue and that you support this issue. Second, you want to become acquainted with the people who are most involved with the campaign and you want them to know you. These are the folks who will likely become staff if your candidate wins and you will want them to know you were a dedicated worker/volunteer during the campaign—and why you worked so hard. Third, even if the candidate loses, many of the campaign workers and staff will go on to work in politics, public policy, or other campaigns, or be candidates themselves. This kind of networking is invaluable. You want to know them and you want them to know you.

Campaigns: Fund-raising

Another way to be active in campaigns is to give money. During the 2012 elections, there was lots of news about Super PACs and the unlimited millions they could spend to get candidates elected. However, there are rules about what individuals can spend in individual elections at the federal and state levels. If donating to a political campaign is going to be part of your citizen lobbyist strategy, you need to know the rules—and where to get the latest updates—because this is an area of law that is experiencing a lot of change.

Federal Campaigns. When donating to federal campaigns themselves, the regulations come from the Federal Election Commission (FEC). According to its Web site, the FEC administers the Federal Election Campaign Act and defends federal campaign law in court. The agency's Web site contains relevant federal law, regulations, and court decisions. This is where you will find the limits on how much an individual can contribute to each federal campaign and to a political party, and other regulations having to do with limits on donations.

Federal Political Action Committees (PACs). After the *Citizens United* decision by the U.S. Supreme Court in 2010, three kinds of PACs existed to support federal campaigns. The first is called a "connected PAC," which is usually established by an organization, business, labor union, or trade group to raise money from a specific group of members or the managers or shareholders of a company. Connected PACs are the most common and are restricted by whom they can receive money from. The second kind of PAC is "unconnected," and these are formed by groups with an ideological purpose, single-issue groups, and political leaders. These unconnected PACs may receive funds from any person, a connected PAC, and corporations. The third and newest type of PAC is the "Super PAC." Created in the wake of the *Citizens United* decision, these are considered "independent-expenditure" PACS. They cannot donate money to political campaigns or political parties and may not work with the campaigns or parties on strategy. However, there are no limits on how much money Super PACs can raise and spend. It is estimated that during the 2012 elections, Super PACs spent more than $546 million.

State Campaign Fund-raising Regulations. Just as there are federal regulations about who can donate and how much can be donated to a campaign or political party, every state has its own and different set of laws and regulations—these are set by the state legislatures and run by the secretary of state or the state board of elections (it varies by state). The FEC, the National Conference of State Legislatures, and the Campaign Finance Institute track state legislation on campaign finance. Among these resources, a citizen lobbyist will be able to find out how much a person can donate to a candidate and a political party—and whether there are any other disclosure requirements. Most of the burden is on the candidates to be open about whom their donors are. So keep in mind that campaign donations are public record, with few exceptions. Each state will also regulate local and state PACs. It should be noted that state and local PACs cannot donate to federal campaigns—only PACs registered with the FEC can donate money to federal campaigns and parties. Finally, in June 2012, the U.S. Supreme Court extended the *Citizens United* decision allowing unlimited independent political spending into the states. The decision overruled Montana's and any other states' laws restricting third-party independent political spending.

Big Fish in a Little Pond

Donating to a political campaign or political party at the

federal, state, or local level can be effective with a donation of just over $200. The reason this is true is because so few Americans actually donate to political causes. According to an analysis of FEC campaign donor disclosure data by Open Secrets, only 0.40 percent of the U.S. population gave more than $200 to political candidates, political parties, or PACs in 2011–12. The FEC requires that federal campaigns, parties, and PACs disclose the names, addresses, occupations, and employers of anyone who contributes $200 or more. These same groups must try to maintain names and addresses on anyone who donates between $50 and $199. The FEC collects this information and makes it public. Every state has its own requirements for reporting donors and expenditures by candidates, political parties, and PACs.

This provides opportunities for a citizen lobbyist who wants to use fund-raising and campaign donations as part of his or her strategy to affect change. Particularly in a local or state political campaign where donors are small and harder to come by, a citizen lobbyist who can mobilize a fund-raiser that brings in a relatively modest amount of money—but that is significant in the donor list of a campaign—makes an opportunity for him- or herself. It is very important to check state campaign laws before taking any action—and even to check with the campaign staff. One popular idea for grassroots efforts is to have someone host a barbecue in a backyard or park. Someone donates the main course (burgers, hot dogs, veggie burgers, chicken, etc.) and everyone else brings a side dish. Then everyone pays a barbecue fee to attend. The barbecue fee then becomes the donation/contribution to the campaign.

Just like the thousand-dollar-a-plate fund-raising dinners that the public often hears about during national campaigns, a smaller grassroots effort may generate local media attention, and it would certainly get the attention of the campaign when the money is turned in. Just be sure to follow all applicable disclosure laws and regulations for the individuals who attend any event or contribute to the event.

11

TO BOLDLY GO—
AND LOBBY

———

The Declaration of Independence was a declaration of war against Great Britain, in part and maybe most importantly because the colonists had sought and been denied representation in Parliament despite being taxed. After the Revolutionary War was over, the United States was created and a new kind of representative democracy was created. I know no one who suggests it is a perfect system or who doesn't have an opinion about how it can be improved.

What is fantastic is that any citizen may comment, complain, and act to change our system of governance from the inside without fear of government reprisal. We have created a multitude of avenues for the citizen lobbyist to take up an issue with public officials in order to effect change.

I have my own strong public policy and political views—but that is not what this guidebook is about. I don't care if you call yourself conservative or liberal; Democrat, Republican, Libertarian, or Green Party; atheist or theist; activist or couch potato; or any other label. My interest in providing this guidebook is to help you and others learn how to be effective citizen lobbyists. The more our citizens engage in public policy and with our elected officials, the more our government—and therefore our society—will benefit.

The more we engage as a people with our public officials, and the more we force our system of governance to answer to us, the better the government works for the people and the better our lives are for it. Let me know how your citizen lobbying efforts go—the good, the interesting, the wacky. I look forward to reading your stories. You can e-mail me at citizenlobbying@gmail.com.

RESOURCE GUIDE

Federal Resources

Campaign Finance Institute: cfinst.org

Federal Election Commission (FEC): fec.gov

Foreign Agents Registration Act (FARA): fara.gov

Internal Revenue Service (IRS): irs.gov

Lobbying Disclosure Act: http://www.senate.gov/legislative/ Lobbying/Lobby_Disclosure_Act/TOC.htm   AND http://lobbyingdisclosure.house.gov/

U.S. House of Representatives: house.gov

U.S. Library of Congress: loc.gov

U.S. Library of Congress, legislative Web site THOMAS: Thomas.loc.gov

U.S. Regulations: regulations.gov

U.S. Senate: senate.gov

State Resources

Campaign Finance Institute: cfinst.org

Federal Election Commission (FEC): fec.gov

National Conference of State Legislatures: ncsl.org

Alabama
- Secretary of State: sos.state.al.us/elections/
- State Legislature: legislature.state.al.us/

Alaska
- Division of Elections: elections.alaska.gov/
- State Legislature: http://w3.legis.state.ak.us/

Arizona
- Secretary of State: azsos.gov/
- State Legislature: azleg.gov/

Arkansas
- Secretary of State: sos.arkansas.gov/Pages/default.aspx
- General Assembly: arkleg.state.ar.us/assembly/2013/2013R/Pages/Home.aspx

California
- Secretary of State: sos.ca.gov/
- State Legislature: legislature.ca.gov/

Colorado
- Secretary of State: sos.state.co.us/
- General Assembly: leg.state.co.us/clics/clics2012B/cslFrontPages.nsf/HomeSplash?OpenForm

Connecticut

- Secretary of State: ct.gov/sots/site/default.asp
- General Assembly: cga.ct.gov/

Delaware
- Commissioner of Elections: elections.delaware.gov/default.shtml
- State Legislature: legis.delaware.gov/

District of Columbia
- Board of Elections & Ethics: dcboee.org/voter_info/register_to_vote/ovr_step1.asp
- Council: dccouncil.washington.dc.us

Florida
- Secretary of State: dos.state.fl.us/
- State Legislature: leg.state.fl.us/Welcome/index.cfm?CFID=281504836&CFTOKEN=71028396

Georgia
- Secretary of State: sos.georgia.gov/
- General Assembly: legis.ga.gov/en-US/default.aspx

Hawaii
- Office of Elections: portal.ehawaii.gov/government/elections-and-voting.html
- State Legislature: capitol.hawaii.gov/

Idaho
- Secretary of State: sos.idaho.gov/
- State Legislature: legislature.idaho.gov/

Illinois
- State Board of Elections: elections.il.gov/
- General Assembly: ilga.gov/

Indiana
- Secretary of State: in.gov/sos/
- General Assembly: in.gov/legislative/

Iowa
- Secretary of State: sos.iowa.gov/
- State Legislature: legis.iowa.gov/index.aspx

Kansas
- Secretary of State: kssos.org/elections/elections.html
- State Legislature: kslegislature.org/li/

Kentucky
- Secretary of State: sos.ky.gov/
- State Legislature: lrc.ky.gov

Louisiana
- Secretary of State: sos.la.gov/
- State Legislature: legis.state.la.us

Maine
- Secretary of State: maine.gov/sos/
- State Legislature: maine.gov/legis/

Maryland
- State Board of Elections: elections.state.md.us/
- General Assembly: mgaleg.maryland.gov/webmga/frm1st.aspx?tab=home

Massachusetts
- Secretary of State: sec.state.ma.us
- General Court: malegislature.gov

Michigan
- Secretary of State: michigan.gov/sos

- State Legislature: legislature.mi.gov

Minnesota
- Secretary of State: sos.state.mn.us
- State Legislature: leg.state.mn.us

Mississippi
- Secretary of State: sos.ms.gov
- State Legislature: billstatus.ls.state.ms.us/

Missouri
- Secretary of State: sos.mo.gov
- General Assembly: moga.mo.gov

Montana
- Secretary of State: sos.mt.gov/
- State Legislature: leg.mt.gov/css/default.asp

Nebraska
- Secretary of State: sos.ne.gov/dyindex.html
- State Legislature: nebraskalegislature.gov/

Nevada
- Secretary of State: nvsos.gov/
- State Legislature: leg.state.nv.us

New Hampshire
- Secretary of State: sos.nh.gov/
- General Court: gencourt.state.nh.us

New Jersey
- Secretary of State: nj.gov/state/
- State Legislature: njleg.state.nj.us

New Mexico
- Secretary of State: sos.state.nm.us

- State Legislature: nmlegis.gov/lcs/

New York
- State Board of Elections: elections.ny.gov
- State Assembly: assembly.state.ny.us/

North Carolina
- State Board of Elections: ncsbe.gov
- General Assembly: ncleg.net

North Dakota
- Secretary of State: nd.gov/sos/
- Legislative Assembly: legis.nd.gov

Ohio
- Secretary of State: sos.state.oh.us
- General Assembly: legislature.state.oh.us

Oklahoma
- State Election Board: ok.gov/elections/
- State Legislature: oklegislature.gov

Oregon
- Secretary of State: sos.state.or.us
- State Legislature: leg.state.or.us

Pennsylvania
- Secretary of State: dos.state.pa.us/portal/server.pt/community/department_of_state/12405
- General Assembly: legis.state.pa.us

Rhode Island
- Secretary of State: sos.ri.gov/
- State Legislature: legislature.state.al.us/

South Carolina

- State Election Commission: scvotes.org
- State Legislature: scstatehouse.gov

South Dakota
- Secretary of State: sdsos.gov/default.aspx
- State Legislature: http://legis.state.sd.us/

Tennessee
- Secretary of State: tn.gov/sos/
- General Assembly: legislature.state.tn.us

Texas
- Secretary of State: sos.state.tx.us
- State Legislature: capitol.state.tx.us

Utah
- Lieutenant Governor: elections.utah.gov
- State Legislature: le.utah.gov/

Vermont
- Secretary of State: sec.state.vt.us
- State Legislature: leg.state.vt.us

Virginia
- Secretary of Commonwealth: commonwealth.virginia.gov/index.cfm (lobbyists only)
- State Board of Elections: sbe.virginia.gov
- General Assembly: virginiageneralassembly.gov/

Washington
- Secretary of State: sos.wa.gov
- State Legislature: leg.wa.gov/pages/home.aspx

West Virginia
- Secretary of State: sos.wv.gov/Pages/default.aspx

- State Legislature: legis.state.wv.us

Wisconsin
- Government Accountability Board: gab.wi.gov/
- State Legislature: legis.wisconsin.gov/Pages/default.aspx

Wyoming
- Secretary of State: soswy.state.wy.us/
- State Legislature: http://legisweb.state.wy.us

APPENDIX I:
SAMPLE LOBBYING PAPER

May 2011

Religious Discrimination in Health Care:
What Congress Can Do

Effective March 25, 2011, the Obama Administration rescinded most of the federal regulation that protects health care professionals who refuse to provide care they find objectionable on moral or religious grounds. The federal regulation established by President George W. Bush was interpreted as shielding workers who refused to participate in particular medical services, such as providing contraceptives to women, treatment for HIV-positive gay men, and in vitro fertilization for lesbian women.

However, new legislation, including H.R. 1179, the Respect the Rights of Conscience Act of 2011, has been introduced in Congress that would allow health care plan issuers to decline coverage of specific medical treatments and services that violate the health care issuer's religious or moral convictions. This is contrary to current federal and state laws that mandate treatments and services for health care plan issuers.

This legislation would also allow any health care provider (i.e. nurse, doctor, pharmacist) to decline to inform a patient about treatments, refuse to participate in a procedure, or acknowledge a specific item or treatment for the benefit of the patient based on the provider's own religious or moral convictions.

According to the U.S. Conference of Catholic Bishops, hospitals, insurers, and health care professionals would be able to refuse to cover or participate in contraceptive care, sterilizations for men and women, abortion and morning-after pills, some types of in vitro fertilization, obligations to treat homosexuals, and legal physician-assisted suicide.

The women of This State are greatly concerned about the chilling effect that such legislation would have on the ability of women to receive comprehensive and quality health care. We must stress the travesty if Congress were to allow health care professionals and health care plan issuers to use religion as a way to deny and obfuscate basic and legitimate health care services to patients who do not share the same religious or moral beliefs.

I, Susan Foreman, on behalf of myself and the 1.2 million women constituents living in This State, urge members of Congress to prevent religious discrimination in health care by:

1. Calling such legislation "religious discrimination" and a "patients' rights" issue instead of a "conscience clause" issue.

2. Voting NO on legislation that would give health care plan issuers and health care providers the rights to deny patients full medical care and information based on their own religious and moral beliefs.

APPENDIX II:
SAMPLE LOBBYING VISIT

Please note that the sample meeting provided here represents a positive interaction.

- **Citizen Lobbyist** walks into Congressional Office. Citizen Lobbyist asks to speak with Staffer, with whom s/he has an appointment.
- **Staffer** comes out and introduces her/himself. "Good morning. I am Jane/Joe Staffer. Thanks for coming today. Please follow me over to this table where we can discuss the issues that brought you here today."
- **Citizen Lobbyist:** "Thank you. I am <u>Harriet Jones from Anywhere USA</u>. I am here today to discuss the following issue(s): <u>Issue 1, Issue 2, and Issue 3</u>."
- **Staffer:** "Great. Do you represent any particular organization or group?"

- **Citizen Lobbyist:** (1) "Yes, I am with <u>Organization X</u>, which is hosting a lobbying day. <u>Organization X</u> is a nonprofit organization that advocates for <u>the rights of nontheists and for the separation of church and state</u>, or (2) No, but I am a concerned voter and active member of my community."

- **Staffer:** "OK, let's get started with the issues that brought you here today."

- **Citizen Lobbyist:** "We'd like the <u>Congressman/woman/ Senator</u> to vote for/against legislation that _____ _____. Shall I tell you a little about our positions on each of these issues?

- **Staffer:** Absolutely. I know about <u>Issue 1</u>, but not so much about <u>Issue 2</u>. I may need to refer you to another staffer on that issue.

- **Citizen Lobbyist:** OK. We have information we will be leaving with you to give to the appropriate person as well as contact information for <u>Organization X</u> if you have any questions about these issues.

  - Discuss <u>Issue 1</u>.

- **Staffer:** "I can't speak for the <u>Congressman/woman/ Senator</u>, but I will be sure to take this information to her/ him.

- **Citizen Lobbyist:** "Thank you. I want you and the Congressman/woman/Senator to know that this is a personal issue for me and for voters back home." *(If able, add a true personal story.)*

- Move on to <u>Issue 2</u>.
- **Staffer:** "Well, this isn't an area that I am familiar with and I may not be the best person, but I can certainly take the information you have."
- **Citizen Lobbyist:** Great.
    - Provide additional details about <u>Issue 2</u>.
- **Staffer:** I didn't know about this. I will certainly pass your concerns on to my colleague and be sure that the <u>Congressman/woman/Senator</u> hears about your visit.
- **Citizen Lobbyist:** Thank you; I appreciate it. Here is the information about the issues I promised to give you. Thank you so much for taking the time to meet with me.
- **Staffer:** Thank you for coming.

If the meeting does not go well, and the interaction proves to be a negative one, remember to always do the following:

- Be courteous to all staff; do not raise your voice or go off-topic
- Reiterate your main points.
- If possible, take notes about why the meeting did not go well. For example, were you treated poorly? Was the issue dismissed as unimportant? Was the meeting canceled?

Did you met with a staffer not connected with the issue? If you are lobbying on your own or with a small group, it will be important to note these issues for future visits. If you are participating in a lobbying day or event organized by a group or organization, be sure to share these observations with the organizations.

NOTES

Introduction

For more about the "anthrax letters" and the tighter security that was instituted in their wake, see "Amerithrax or Anthrax Investigation," Federal Bureau of Investigation (FBI), www.fbi.gov/about-us/history/famous-cases/anthrax-amerithrax; "Capitol Security Changes since 9/11," *Roll Call*, September 7, 2011, www.rollcall.com/media/newspics/090711security graphic.pdf; and "9/11 Impacts Security at the Statehouse," Rhode Island Public Radio, www.publicbroadcasting.net/wrni/news.newsmain/article/0/13/1851078/Top.Stories/911. impacts.security.at.the.statehouse.

According to then–U.S. representative Tim Scott's congressional Web site, security screening for letters can take an additional two weeks. See http://timscott.house.gov/office/washington-dc, December 27, 2012. According to the Web site of Washington Express, a District of

Columbia courier service, mail sent to congressional offices is subject to "inspection, quarantine, and irradiation." See http://www.washingtonexpress.com/services/documents/capitolhilldeliverycapabilities.pdf.

For media reports about the turnout for the 2008 presidential elections and President Obama's call to "make your voice heard," see "2009 Election Turnout Hit 40-Year High," *CBS News*, June 18, 2009, www.cbsnews.com/2100-250_162-4670319.html, and "Phones Swamped, Servers Crash as Voters Slam Congress," *CNNPolitics.com*, July 26, 2011, www.cnn.com/2011/POLITICS/07/26/congress.communications.jammed/index.html.

Chapter 1

It should be noted that some mayors are appointed from among the elected city council members and that some cities or towns may use the commission form of municipal government or city manager model. You should check with your local officials to determine how officials are elected or appointed and the basis for citizen representation in your area.

When writing to a newspaper, be sure to check the requirements for letters to the editor carefully before submitting yours. Many letters are restricted by word content, format, etc. Don't get disqualified by a technicality!

"Amerithrax" is the case name for the anthrax investigation

used by the FBI. For more, see "Amerithrax or Anthrax Investigation," FBI, www.fbi.gov/about-us/history/famous-cases/anthrax-amerithrax.

The quote from Justice Brandeis can be found in "What Publicity Can Do," *Harper's Weekly*, 1913.

For more on CEO pay, see Scott DeCarlo, "Gravity-Defying CEO Compensation," *Forbes*, April 4, 2012, www.forbes.com/lists/2012/12/ceo-compensation-12_land.html. The three most highly paid CEOs are (1) John H. Hammergren (McKesson); (2) Ralph Lauren (Ralph Lauren); (3) Michael D. Fascitelli (Vornado Realty).

For the pay of U.S. politicians and elected officials, see "The Ten-Highest Paid Government Jobs," *Wall Street Journal*, March 4, 2011, http://247wallst.com/2011/03/04/the-ten-highest-paid-government-jobs/2/; Mark Kurlyandchik, "Ranking Local Government Leaders' Salaries," *Hour Detroit*, February 2012, www.hourdetroit.com/Hour-Detroit/February-2012/Pay-for-Pols/; "On Average, Governors' Salaries Show Decline in Pay," *Stateline*, April 7, 2011, www.pewstates.org/projects/stateline/headlines/on-average-governors-salaries-show-decline-in-pay-85899375094; and 2012 NCSL Legislator Compensation and Per Diem Table, National Conference of State Legislatures, www.ncsl.org/legislatures-elections/legisdata/2012-ncsl-legislator-compensation-data.aspx.

Chapter 2

The information about IRS rules toward lobbying and its definition of "legislation" comes from the IRS Web site. See "Lobbying," www.irs.gov/Charities-&-Non-Profits/Lobbying (accessed September 23, 2012).

For more about the IRS's tests for lobbying by nonprofit organizations, see "Measuring Lobbying: Substantial Part Test," IRS, www.irs.gov/Charities-&-Non-Profits/Measuring-Lobbying:--Substantial-Part-Test (accessed September 23, 2012), and "Measuring Lobbying Activity: Expenditure Test," IRS, www.irs.gov/Charities-&-Non-Profits/Measuring-Lobbying-Activity:--Expenditure-Test (accessed September 23, 2012).

For more about the rules surrounding the registration of foreign lobbyists and the number of countries with registered foreign agents in the United States, see Foreign Agents Registration Act (FARA), www.fara.gov/, and "Report of the Attorney General to the Congress of the United States on the Administration of the Foreign Agents Registration Act of 1938, as Amended, for the Six Months Ending December 31, 2011," FARA, www.fara.gov/.

For a complete list of definitions and descriptions related to domestic lobbying, visit the Web site of the U.S. Senate, http://www.senate.gov/legislative/Lobbying/Lobby_Disclosure_Act/3_Definitions.htm.

For information about registering as a lobbyist in your state, visit "Lobbyist Registration Requirements," National Conference of State Legislatures, February 2012, www.ncsl. org/legislatures-elections/ethicshome/50-state-chart-lobbyist-registration-requirements.aspx.

Chapter 3

The referenced congressional bills were the Homeless Children and Youth Act of 2011, H.R. 32 (2011), and the Ronald Reagan Commemorative Coin Act of 2011, H.R. 497 (2011).

The Web address for the Library of Congress's Web site THOMAS is Thomas.loc.gov.

Chapter 8

The book by Barbour and Koneya was published by Merrill in 1976. Even if the percentages given are not fully accurate, the takeaway is the same: how you act and present yourself in a meeting is as important to your message as what you say.

Chapter 10

For information about the electoral college, try these books: Tara Ross, *Enlightened Democracy: The Case for the Electoral College*, 2nd ed. (Dallas, TX: Colonial Press, 2012); George C. Edwards III, *Why the Electoral College Is Bad for America*, 2nd ed. (New Haven, CT: Yale University Press, 2011).

For more about the electoral challenges America still faces, see Joseph Stiglitz, *The Price of Inequality: How Today's Divided Society Endangers Our Future* (New York: W. W. Norton & Company, 2012); Christopher Hayes, *Twilight of the Elites: America after Meritocracy* (New York: Crown, June 2012).

To request voter information from the state of Florida, visit "Monthly Voter File Request for Information, Florida Division of Elections," http://election.dos.state.fl.us/voter-registration/Voter_File_Request_for_Info.shtml (accessed January 1, 2013).

For information about accessing voter information in Iowa, visit "Voter Registration List Requests," Research and Data, Iowa Secretary of State, http://sos.iowa.gov/elections/otherinfo.html (accessed January 1, 2013).

For more about the question I posed to President Obama, see "Secular Coalition Presses Obama on Faith-Based Policies During Live Town Hall Meeting, Secular Coalition for America," July 22, 2011, http://secular.org/content/secular-coalition-presses-obama-faith-based-policies-during-live-town-hall-meeting.

For more about campaign finance laws and filing requirements, see "Federal Campaign Finance Laws," Federal Election Commission, http://www.fec.gov; "Code of Federal Regulations," FEC, http://www.fec.gov/law/cfr/cfr_2009.pdf;

and "Chart 1: Campaign Finance Report Filing Requirements," FEC, www.fec.gov/pubrec/cfl/cfl98/chart1.html.

The *Citizens United* case is officially known as *Citizens United v. Federal Election Commission*, 558 U.S. 310 (2010).

Information about Super PAC spending in the 2012 elections comes from "Super PAC Spending," *Los Angeles Times*, November 20, 2012, http://graphics.latimes.com/2012-election-superpac-spending/ (accessed January 1, 2013).

For more about state fund-raising regulations, see "Chart 1: Campaign Finance Report Filing Requirements," Federal Election Commission (FEC), http://www.fec.gov/pubrec/cfl/cfl98/chart1.html; National Conference of State Legislatures, www.ncsl.org/; and "State Links," Campaign Finance Institute, www.cfinst.org/law/stateLinks.aspx

The U.S. Supreme Court case that extended the *Citizens United* decision to allow unlimited independent political spending into the states was *American Tradition Partnership v. Bullock*, No. 11–1179, June 25, 2012.

For eye-opening data about the breakdown of campaign contributions, see "Donor Demographics, 2012 Overview," Opensecrets.org, http://www.opensecrets.org/overview/donor demographics.php.

INDEX

ABOUT THE AUTHOR

Amanda Knief is a public policy and constitutional expert on religious freedom and civil liberties. She has worked as a legal counsel and legislative drafter for the Iowa Legislature and the lobbyist for the Secular Coalition for America, and is currently the managing director and in-house counsel for American Atheists. She has a JD from Drake University Law School and a BS in journalism and science communication from Iowa State University.

OTHER TITLES FROM PITCHSTONE

———————

Candidate Without a Prayer:
An Autobiography of a Jewish Atheist in the Bible Belt
by Herb Silverman

PsychoBible:
Behavior, Religion & the Holy Book
by Armando Favazza, MD

What You Don't Know about Religion
(but should)
by Ryan T. Cragun

Why Are You Atheists So Angry?:
99 Things That Piss Off the Godless
by Greta Christina

Why We Believe in God(s):
A Concise Guide to the Science of Faith
by J. Anderson Thomson, Jr., MD, with Clare Aukofer